Every day four old men
met under a mango tree.
The four old men sat on four old chairs,
and talked and talked and talked.
They were very good friends.

The four old men were all blind.
They had eyes, but they could not see.
They could not see flowers or trees
in the yard.
They could not see dogs or cats
in the road.
Children jumped and ran,
but the four blind men could not see them.
Mothers walked to market,
but the four blind men could not see them.
Girls played, and boys threw stones,
but the four blind men could not see them.
Because they were blind and could not see,
the four old men sat and talked all day.
They were friends, and they were happy.

4

The four blind men could not see,
but they were old, and knew many things.
They knew things which the chief did not know.
They knew things which the teacher did not know.
They knew things which the doctor did not know.
But the four blind men did not know one thing.
They did not know what an elephant was.

Every day they sat under the mango tree,
and talked and talked and talked,
but they did not know what an elephant was.
"Can it run or jump or walk?"
asked the first blind man.
"Is it red or yellow or brown or white?"
asked the second blind man.
"Is it big or small or old or new?"
asked the third blind man.
"Has it got four or six or eight or ten legs?"
asked the fourth blind man.
They talked and talked and talked,
but they did not know what an elephant was.

One hot Monday afternoon
the four blind men sat under the mango tree.
They talked and talked and talked,
but they did not know what an elephant was.
A small boy sat behind them. He said,
"I saw an elephant this morning.
If I take you to the elephant
you can touch it.
Then you will know what an elephant is.
Who will come with me?"

"Take me, take me, I want to go,"
said the first blind man.
"No, I must go. I am older than you,"
said the second blind man.
"No, I must go. I am bigger than you,"
said the third blind man.
"No, I must go. I can walk faster than you,"
said the fourth blind man.

"Today is Monday," said the small boy.
"We will go tomorrow. Do not forget.
I will take you to the elephant tomorrow."

On Tuesday morning the four blind men
met the small boy under the mango tree.
"You must take me to the elephant today,"
said the first blind man.
"My friends can go tomorrow."
"Give me your hand so you do not fall,"
the small boy said to him.

The first blind man and the small boy
walked down the road and through the trees.
They were hot and dirty,
and they wanted some water,
but they walked on and on.
Then the small boy stopped.
"What is it?" asked the first blind man.
"Where are we? Where is the elephant?
Is it in the river or behind the trees?
Will it bite me or kick me?
My eyes cannot see this thing. I am afraid."
"Here is the elephant," said the small boy.
"We will walk round the elephant,
and then you can touch it."

The elephant was asleep.
The small boy and the blind man
walked round the elephant,
and then the small boy said,
"If you put out your hand
you can touch the elephant now."

The first blind man put out his hand.
"What is this thing?" he asked,
and he touched the elephant.
Then he knew what an elephant was.
"A spear, a spear," he said.
"An elephant is a spear.
An elephant is a big spear,
and a man can throw it.
Take me to my friends. I must tell them.
An elephant is a big spear,
and a man can throw it.
I must run and tell my friends."

The first blind man and the small boy
ran as fast as they could.
The friends sat under the mango tree.
"I touched it," said the first blind man.
"I touched the elephant.
Now I can tell you what an elephant is.
An elephant is a big spear,
and a man can throw it.
Do not forget. An elephant is a spear."
"A spear?" asked his friends. "No, no.
An elephant is not a spear,
and a man cannot throw it."

The four blind men talked all afternoon.
"An elephant is a big spear."
"No, it is not. An elephant is not a spear."
"Yes it is. I tell you, an elephant is a spear."

They did not ask the small boy,
"What is an elephant?"
and he did not tell them.
When it was night they all walked home.

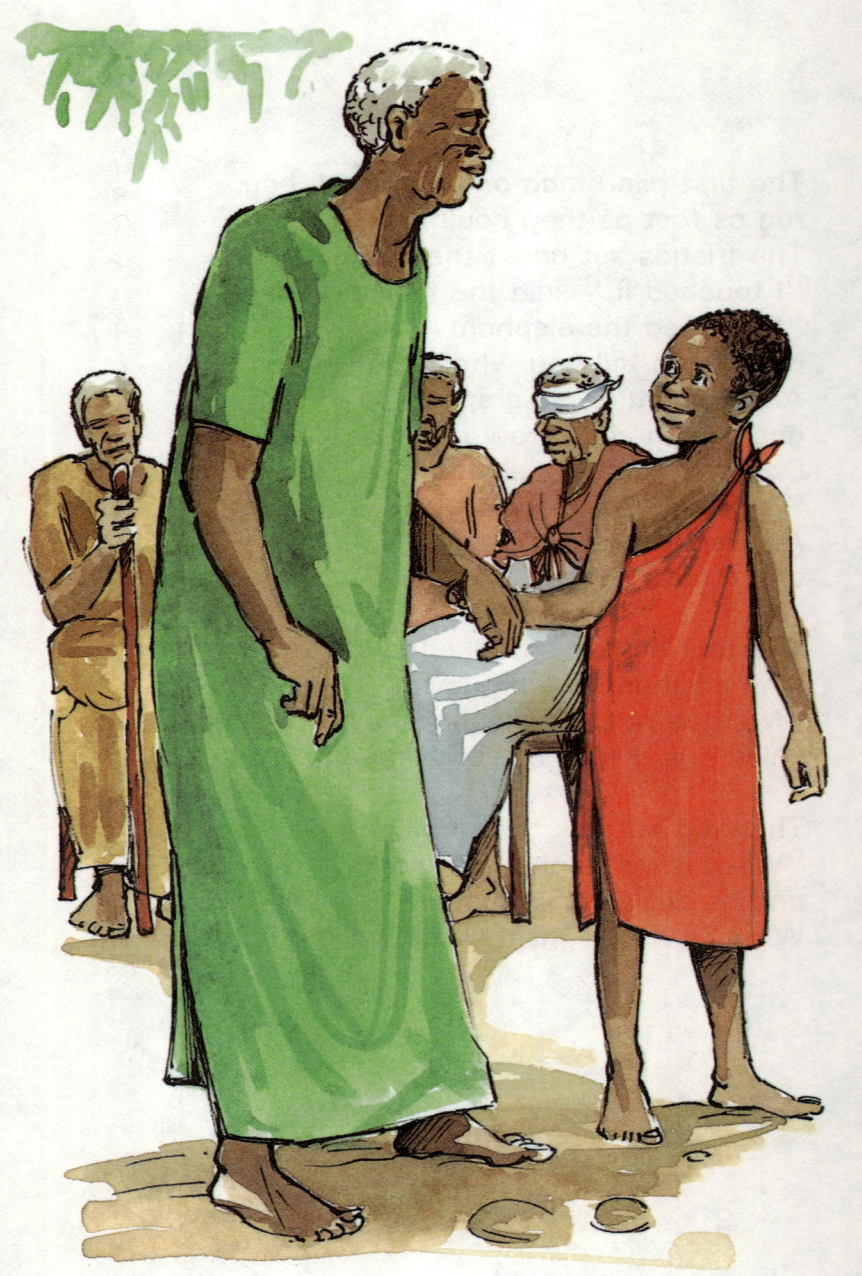

On Wednesday morning the four blind men
met the small boy under the mango tree.
"You must take me to the elephant today,"
said the second blind man.
"You took my friend yesterday,
and I want to go today."
"Give me your hand so you do not fall,"
the small boy said to him.

The second blind man and the small boy
walked down the road and through the trees.
They were hot and dirty,
and they wanted some water,
but they walked on and on.
Then the small boy stopped.
"What is it?" asked the second blind man.
"Where are we? Where is the elephant?
Is it in the river or behind the trees?
Will it cut me or hurt me?
My eyes cannot see this thing. I am afraid."
"Here is the elephant," said the small boy.
"We will walk round the elephant,
and then you can touch it."

The elephant was asleep.
The small boy and the second blind man
walked round the elephant,
and then the small boy said,
"If you put out your hand
you can touch the elephant now."

The second blind man put out his hand.
"What is this thing?" he asked,
and he touched the elephant.
Then he knew what an elephant was.
"A rope, a rope," he said.
"An elephant is a rope.
An elephant is a big rope,
and a man can tie it.
Take me to my friends. I must tell them.
An elephant is a big rope,
and a man can tie it.
It is not a spear. It is a rope.
I must run and tell my friends."

The second blind man and the small boy
ran as fast as they could.
The friends sat under the mango tree.
"I touched it," said the second blind man.
"I touched the elephant,
and now I can tell you what it is.
An elephant is a big rope,
and a man can tie it.
Do not forget. An elephant is a rope."
"No it is not," said the first blind man.
"An elephant is a spear,
and a man can throw it.
An elephant is not a rope,
and a man cannot tie it."

The four blind men talked all afternoon.
"I tell you, an elephant is a rope."
"No it is not. It is a spear."
"I touched it. It is not a spear."
"I touched it too. It is not a rope."

They did not ask the small boy,
"What is an elephant?"
and he did not tell them.
When it was night they all walked home.

On Thursday morning the four blind men
met the small boy under the mango tree.
The third blind man said,
"Take me to the elephant please.
You took my friend yesterday,
and I want to go today."
"Give me your hand so you do not fall,"
the small boy said to him.

The third blind man and the small boy
walked down the road and through the trees.
They were hot and dirty,
and they wanted some water,
but they walked on and on.
Then the small boy stopped.
"What is it?" asked the third blind man.
"Where are we? Where is the elephant?
Is it in the river or behind the trees?
Is it as big as a house
or as small as a mouse?
My eyes cannot see this thing. I am afraid."
"Here is the elephant," said the small boy.
"We will walk round the elephant,
and then you can touch it."

The elephant was asleep.
The small boy and the blind man
walked round the elephant,
and then the small boy said,
"If you put out your hand
you can touch the elephant now."

The third blind man put out his hand.
"What is this thing?" he asked,
and he touched the elephant.
Then he knew what an elephant was.
"A door, a door," he said.
"An elephant is a door.
An elephant is a big door,
and a man can shut it.
Take me to my friends. I must tell them.
An elephant is a big door,
and a man can shut it.
It is not a spear or a rope.
I must run and tell my friends."

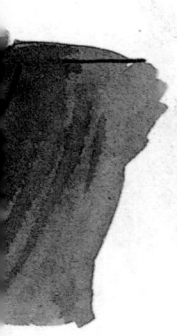

The third man and the small boy
ran as fast as they could.
The friends sat under the mango tree.
"I touched it," said the third blind man.
"Now I can tell you what an elephant is.
An elephant is a big door,
and a man can shut it.
Do not forget. An elephant is a door."

The four blind men talked all afternoon.
"I tell you, an elephant is a door,
and a man can shut it."
"No it is not. An elephant is a spear,
and a man can throw it."
"No, no. An elephant is a rope,
and a man can tie it."

They did not ask the small boy,
"What is an elephant?"
and he did not tell them.
When it was night they all walked home.

On Friday morning the four blind men
met the small boy under the mango tree.
"Please take me to the elephant today,"
said the fourth blind man.
"You took my friend yesterday,
and I want to go today."
"Give me your hand so you do not fall,"
the small boy said to him.

The fourth blind man and the small boy
walked down the road and through the trees.
They were hot and dirty,
and they wanted some water,
but they walked on and on.
Then the small boy stopped.
"What is it?" asked the fourth blind man.
"Where are we? Where is the elephant?
Is it in the river or behind the trees?
Is it magic? Is it a monster?
My eyes cannot see this thing. I am afraid."
"Here is the elephant," said the small boy.
"We will walk round the elephant,
and then you can touch it."

The elephant was asleep.
The small boy and the fourth blind man
walked round the elephant,
and then the small boy said,
"If you put out your hand
you can touch the elephant now."

The fourth blind man put out his hand.
"What is this thing?" he asked,
and he touched the elephant.
Then he knew what an elephant was.
"A snake, a snake," he said.
"An elephant is a snake.
An elephant is a big snake,
and a man can cut the head off with a knife.
Take me to my friends. I must tell them.
An elephant is a snake,
and a man can cut the head off with a knife.
It is not a spear or a rope or a door.
I must run and tell my friends."

The fourth blind man and the small boy
ran as fast as they could.
The friends sat under the mango tree.
"I touched it," said the fourth blind man.
"I touched the elephant,
and now I can tell you what it is.
An elephant is a big snake,
and a man can cut the head off with a knife.
Do not forget. An elephant is a snake."
"A snake?" asked his friends. "A snake?
No, no. An elephant is not a snake.
A man cannot cut the head off with a knife."

The four blind men talked all afternoon.
"I tell you, an elephant is a snake,
and a man can cut the head off with a knife."
"No it is not. An elephant is a door,
and a man can shut it."
"No, no. An elephant is a rope,
and a man can tie it."
"No, no, no. An elephant is a spear,
and a man can throw it."

They did not ask the small boy,
"What is an elephant?"
and he did not tell them.
When it was night they all walked home.

The four blind men met under the mango tree
on Saturday and on Sunday too.
The four old friends sat on four old chairs,
and talked and talked and talked.
They talked in the morning.
They talked in the afternoon.
They talked at night.

But they did not know what an elephant was.
They did not ask the small boy,
and the small boy did not tell them.